KIDS AROUND the WORLD

The World's Wonders

By Gloria Cruz
Illustrations by Clarice Elliott

Ready-to-Read

SIMON SPOTLIGHT • An imprint of Simon & Schuster Children's Publishing Division • New York Amsterdam/Antwerp London Toronto Sydney/Melbourne New Delhi • 1230 Avenue of the Americas, New York, New York 10020 • For more than 100 years, Simon & Schuster has championed authors and the stories they create. By respecting the copyright of an author's intellectual property, you enable Simon & Schuster and the author to continue publishing exceptional books for years to come. We thank you for supporting the author's copyright by purchasing an authorized edition of this book. No amount of this book may be reproduced or stored in any format, nor may it be uploaded to any website, database, language-learning model, or other repository, retrieval, or artificial intelligence system without express permission. All rights reserved. Inquiries may be directed to Simon & Schuster, 1230 Avenue of the Americas, New York, NY 10020 or permissions@simonandschuster.com. • This Simon Spotlight edition September 2025 • Text © 2025 by Simon & Schuster, LLC • Illustrations © 2025 by Clarice Elliott • All rights reserved, including the right of reproduction in whole or in part in any form. SIMON SPOTLIGHT, READY-TO-READ, and colophon are registered trademarks of Simon & Schuster, LLC. For information about special discounts for bulk purchases, please contact Simon & Schuster Special Sales at 1-866-506-1949 or business@simonandschuster.com. Simon & Schuster strongly believes in freedom of expression and stands against censorship in all its forms. For more information, visit BooksBelong.com. The Simon & Schuster Speakers Bureau can bring authors to your live event. For more information or to book an event contact the Simon & Schuster Speakers Bureau at 1-866-248-3049 or visit our website at www.simonspeakers.com. • Manufactured in the United States of America 0725 LAK • 2 4 6 8 10 9 7 5 3 1 • CIP data for this book is available from the Library of Congress. ISBN 9781665973274 (hc) • ISBN 9781665973267 (pbk) • ISBN 9781665973281 (ebook)

Glossary

archaeologists: scientists who study items of past human life and activities, such as tools, pottery, jewelry, stone walls, and monuments

architects: people who design and plan the construction of buildings or structures

centennial: a one hundredth anniversary

climate change: major and long-lasting changes in temperatures and weather patterns

geoglyphs: large, man-made marks created by arranging or removing landscape to create an image or shape

geology: the study of the history of the earth as recorded in rocks

Indigenous: relating to the earliest people known to live in a place

millennium: a period of one thousand years

pharaohs: rulers from ancient Egypt

prehistoric: relating to, or existing in, times before written history

Note to readers: Some of these words may have more than one definition. The definitions above match how these words are used in this book.

Contents

Note to readers: There are wonders all around our world! These are just a few of the most well-known landmarks.

Chapter 1:
A Long Time Ago

In every corner of the world you can find unique structures called landmarks. Landmarks are recognizable features or objects that hold meaning for people.

Before modern cities and towering skyscrapers, there were ancient monuments built thousands of years ago, and man-made landmarks that could be seen from the sky. How some of these wonders came to be is still a mystery.

In Egypt the Giza Pyramids
(say: GEE-zuh PEER-uh-muhdz)
have towered over the Sahara
Desert for over 4,500 years!
These pyramids were built as
tombs for three **pharaohs**
(say: FAIR-ohs).

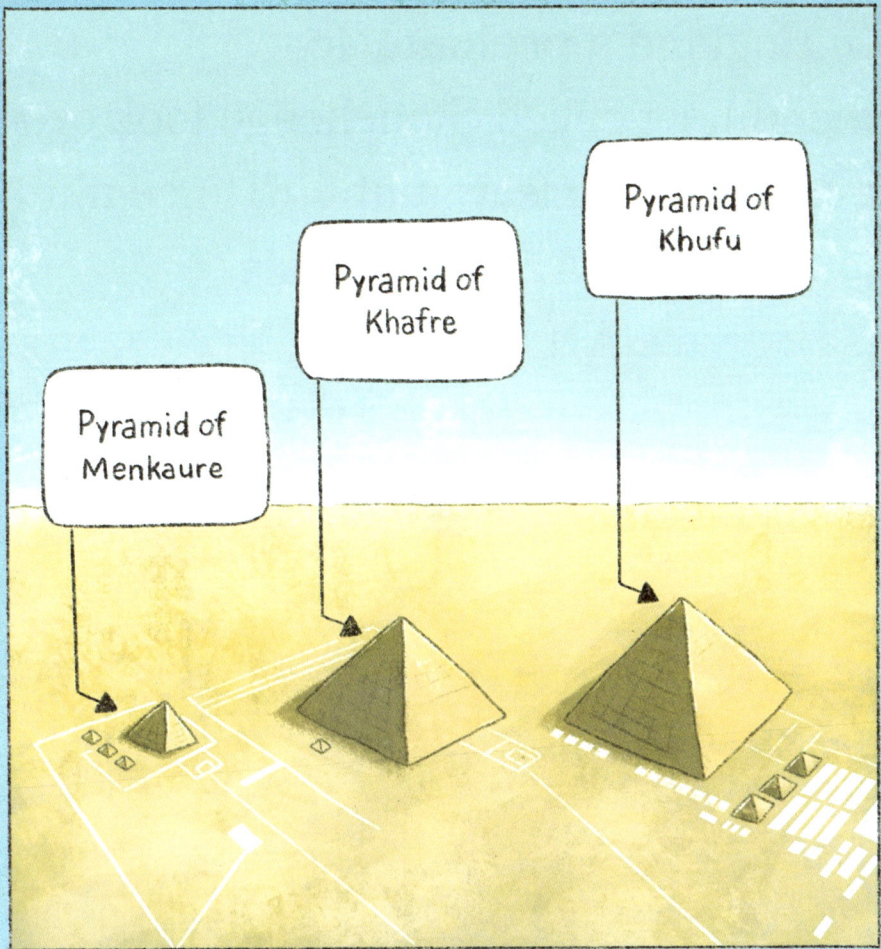

The Great Pyramid is the largest, and it served as the tomb for Pharaoh Khufu. Scientists believe about 2.3 million stone blocks were used to build it!

In England a **prehistoric** monument called Stonehenge took over a **millennium** (say: muh-LEH-nee-uhm) to construct! **Archaeologists** (say: ar-kee-AH-luh-justs) are still not sure how it was created or what it was used for.

The biggest stone weighs about
thirty tons. The smaller stones have
been traced to a part of Wales
that is about 150 miles away!

In Peru there is a collection of images on the ground called **geoglyphs** (say: JEE-oh-gliffs). Over two thousand years ago, **Indigenous** (say: in-DIH-juh-nuss) Nazca people created them by removing stones from the ground and revealing the lighter-colored dirt underneath.

There are over three hundred Nazca geoglyphs, and the best way to see them is from the sky!

The Great Wall of China is a structure that was built over nine Chinese dynasties and took centuries to complete.

It is more than thirteen thousand miles long and was originally built to keep out invaders.

In Athens, Greece, there is a temple made of marble called the Parthenon (say: PAR-thuh-naan). This grand temple was dedicated to Athena, the goddess of war, wisdom, and crafts.

Today, the ruins are white,
but traces of paint suggest
that the temple may have
been originally painted in
vivid colors like blue and red.

Chapter 2:
Reach for the Sky

As technology advanced, man-made landmarks became even more spectacular! For example, the tallest building in the world is currently the Burj Khalifa (say: BURJ kuh-LEE-fuh) in Dubai.

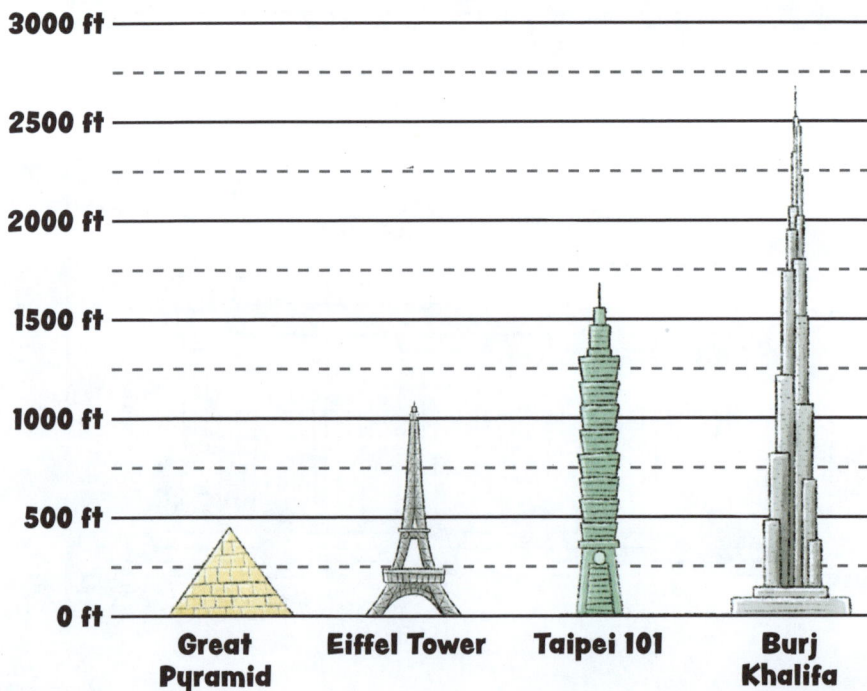

3000 ft	
2500 ft	
2000 ft	
1500 ft	
1000 ft	
500 ft	
0 ft	

| Great Pyramid | Eiffel Tower | Taipei 101 | Burj Khalifa |

The Burj Khalifa is 2,717 feet tall and took six years to build. However, people are always trying to build taller towers. One day, there might even be a tower taller than the Burj Khalifa!

Paris is known for its Iron Lady,
the Eiffel Tower
(say: EYE-fuhl TAU-ur).
Made up of over eighteen thousand
iron pieces bolted together,
it stands at 1,083 feet tall!

The tower was built in 1889
as a **centennial**
(say: suhn-TEH-nee-uhl)
monument for the French Revolution.
Today it holds restaurants and exhibits,
and it has a seventeen-foot-tall antenna
at the top.

Italian **architects** (say: AAR-kuh-tekts) designed the Tower of Pisa (say: PEE-zuh) in 1173. People noticed its leaning position after the first three stories were constructed. The leaning was caused by the soft ground it was built on.

Towers have many purposes,
such as telling time or sending
radio signals. The Tower of Hercules,
(say: HUR-kyuh-leez) in A Coruña,
Spain, is the oldest lighthouse
that is still active today.
It is about two thousand years old!

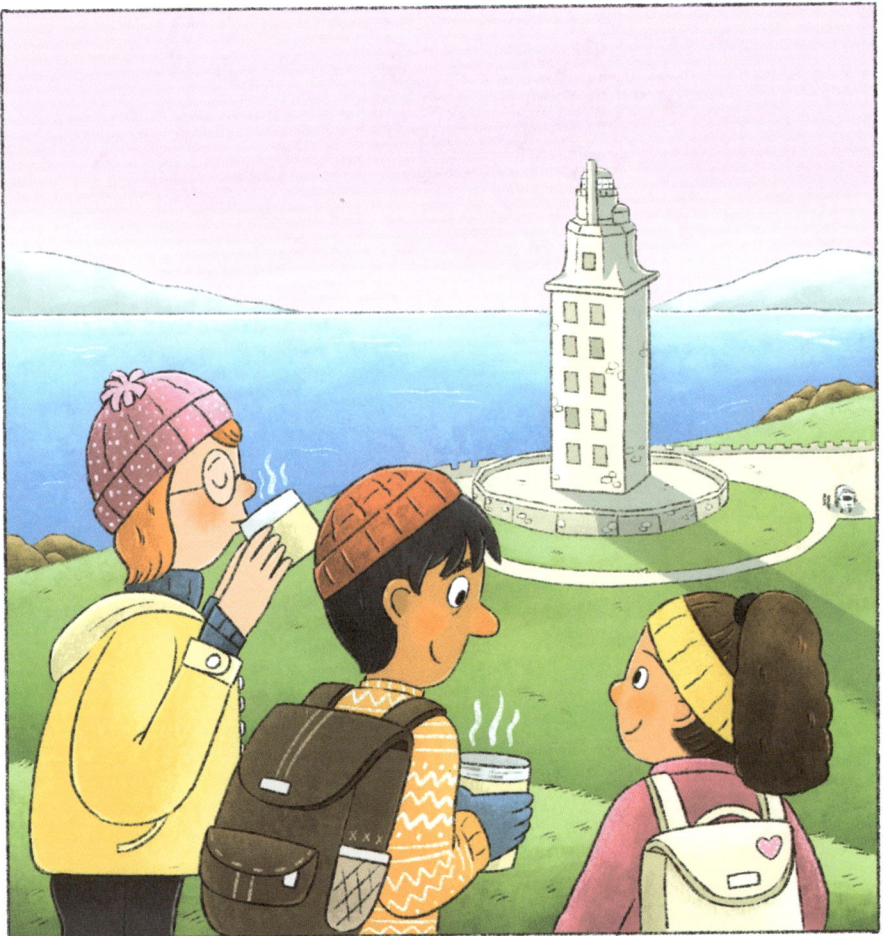

Chapter 3:
Natural Wonders

Man-made landmarks are fascinating, but there are also wonders created by nature!

Victoria Falls is the largest waterfall in the world! Falling between Zambia and Zimbabwe, it is one of the few places in the world where moonbows, or moonlight rainbows, occur.

Mount Fuji is an active volcano in Japan and is the tallest peak in the country. More than three hundred thousand people climb Mount Fuji every year!
It can take up to ten hours to climb to the summit.

Mount Fuji is a significant cultural icon in Japan and has been featured in famous artworks such as the Thirty-Six Views of Mount Fuji by the artist Katsushika Hokusai.

The layers of rock that make up the Grand Canyon in Arizona in the United States can tell us a lot about the history of the Earth.

By studying the Grand Canyon's **geology** (say: jee-AH-luh-jee), such as fossils and rocks, scientists can understand what the region was like over millenniums.

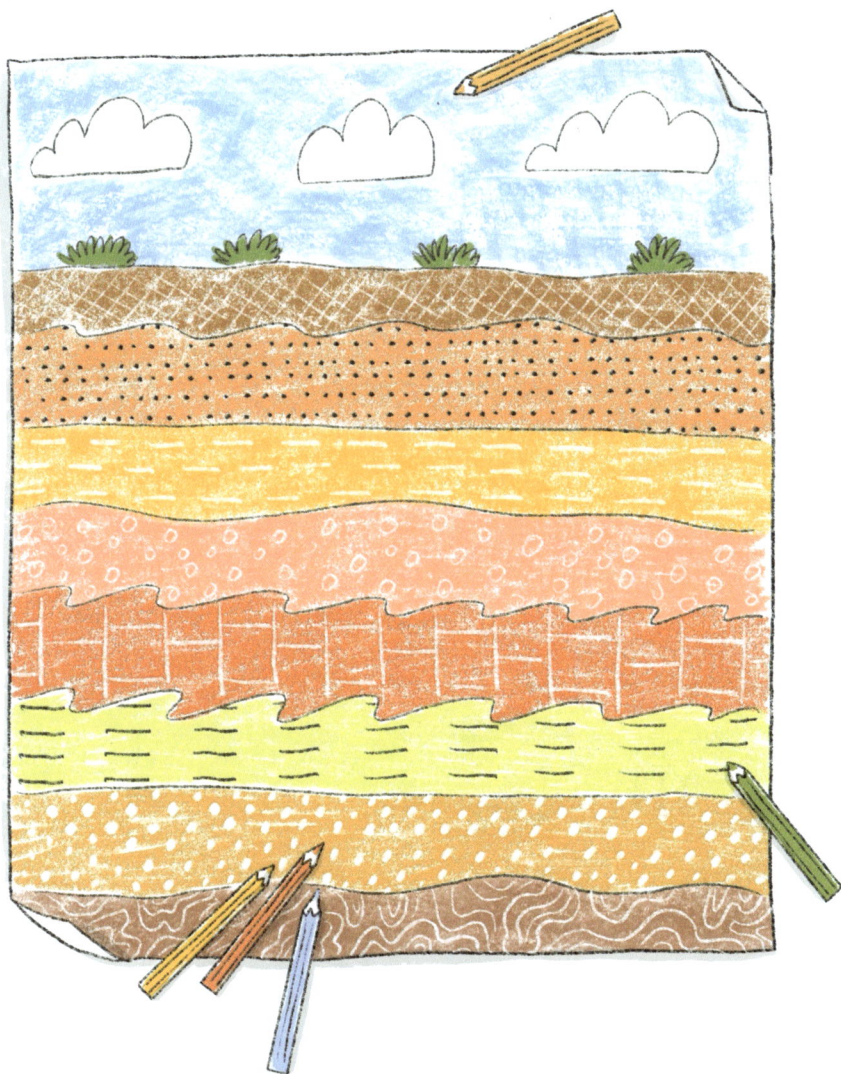

Australia is home to the Great Barrier Reef (GBR), a coral reef system and the largest living structure on earth. Nearly nine thousand animal species can be found here!

The reef and its creatures are at risk of decline due to **climate change**. Scientists and people just like you are doing their part to save the GBR!

Landmarks teach us about the world, its history, and the people living in it.

These are just some of the
world's amazing wonders.
There are so many more to see!
Have you ever visited
a famous landmark?

22.26.25 ▶ 1320 660A 41660907

17.12.18 ▶ 960 320A 325290:12

Build Your Own Tower!

Throughout history, people have tried to build the tallest towers. Now it's your turn! All you need is the following:

- **an adult to help you**
- **wooden Popsicle sticks**
- **crayons or markers**
- **glue**

Use the wooden Popsicle sticks and glue to build a miniature tower, then decorate it with crayons or markers. Here are some ideas to get you started:

- Does your tower lean like the Tower of Pisa?

- Does it have an antenna like the Eiffel Tower?

- Is there a light inside like a lighthouse?

Your tower could be the next great wonder of the world!